Acclaim for Process M

Survey Comments from W

C000051165

Very practical, well presented, easy to understand,
able to communicate to team and put to work right away.

Dynamic and interesting presenter.

Very poignant topic for most, if not all, organizations.

Extremely well done!
Polished, engaging and very worthwhile.

This is a 10.

Very engaging and user friendly presentation.

Very informative.

It will help me improve business processes.

One of the best sessions I attended during the conference!
This was similar to a TED talk.

Very useful! I'll use these tips in my work life.

I appreciated how practical this was.

Very good session and instructor was super.

Excellent, clear, practical presentation.

He's a great, dynamic presenter.

Great examples and context.
Very much applicable to my current work.

Feel I can go do a process mapping exercise.

His tips, tricks and nuances around the RACI model
were extremely timely for me.

Very helpful steps.
Learned how to create a work flow.

Excellent, engaging, interesting, motivating.

Great content, presentation.

Clear to understand presentation. Great presenter.

Great instructor. Very engaging.

Ideas very applicable to work.

Very engaging and informational session.
It's my favorite session so far.

Great tips and easy to follow steps.

Awesome sauce!

Process Mapping Road Trip

Improve organizational workflow in five steps

William Sparks

Title: Process Mapping Road Trip

Subtitle: Improve organizational workflow in five steps

Author: William Sparks

Published by: Promptitude Publishing in Denton, Maryland.

Cover design: William Sparks

Street signs on front cover created at www.wigflip.com/EasyStreet. Illustrations
and street sign images in diagrams 2, 4-8 and back cover courtesy of
www.pixaby.com.

First Edition, 2016

ISBN #978-0-692-76835-8

Published in the United States of America

10 9 8 7 6 5 4 3 2 1

For Jennifer and Vienna,

Let the adventure continue

"Progress isn't made by early risers.
It's made by lazy men trying to find
easier ways to do something."

~Robert A. Heinlein

"What would you say you do here?"

~Bob Slydell, Office Space

Table of Contents

About the Author

Winner of the Dr. J.P. London Award for Promoting Ethical Behavior, William Sparks has over twenty years of management and international development experience in building organizational capacity throughout Africa, Asia, South America, and Europe.

He co-developed the AchieVe Performance Management System, which was selected as an Innovation finalist in the HR Leadership Awards. His international work included the creation of Sell More For More, a capacity development program for cooperative organizations in the least developed countries. Launched in Rwanda, Sell More For More has since expanded to over ten countries. The program was named by InterAction and IFAD as a Best Practice for international development.

A dynamic public speaker, William routinely conducts workshops on improving organizational performance. This book is based on a highly acclaimed session presented annually at the global InsideNGO Conference, which also awarded him the Operational Excellence Award for his contributions over the years in developing international NGOs.

He currently serves as Senior Vice President of Strategic Initiatives at ACDI/VOCA (www.acdivoca.org), an international organization building social and economic opportunities in over 40 countries. William earned his Masters of Science in Organization Development from Pepperdine University.

For relaxation, William is an ultra-marathon runner who runs every morning in whichever country he finds himself that day.

Foreword

You just never know where life will lead you. When a group of us in our twenties founded InsideNGO almost forty years ago, our idea was to bring NGOs together to share experiences, gain knowledge, and learn from each other. Our hope was to help each other out and thereby benefit our organizations all of whom were seeking to make the world a better place for those less fortunate, underprivileged, or just simply in need. InsideNGO created a venue for NGOs to learn together and to pay it forward.

The book in your hand is an example of just that.

Whether or not you work at an NGO, organizations struggle with getting things done. We have processes that convert limited resources into work valued by society, and these processes create the unique DNA of each organization.

As I have watched InsideNGO grow into an association of 350 organizations, I have witnessed the complexity of our organizations increase dramatically. Ever-increasing government regulations, a growing emphasis on measuring impact, a renewed focus on the triple bottom line, and a push for a shared value proposition that includes partnerships with all types of organizations: private sector firms, government agencies, research universities, and non-profit organizations, are pressures we all experience. Work is becoming more complex. With it, processes stretch across departments, time zones, and even organizational boundaries.

So it is timely that William has shared his approach to process mapping. He has been a favorite presenter at our Annual Conference in Washington, D.C. for several years as well as at workshops both in the United States and overseas. His sessions, particularly his workshop on process mapping, receive the highest of ratings. He has a unique and humorous way of breaking down complex topics into memorable and easy frameworks. His analogy of process mapping as a family road trip is one such example. It is a journey that I trust you will enjoy.

Recently, William was awarded the InsideNGO Operational Excellence Award. This is an honor we do not give lightly. Through work in his own organization and his contributions to the NGO community through InsideNGO, he continues to share his insights. While I couldn't have predicted when we began that I would be writing these words almost forty years later, I have always known that the power of people working together would produce meaningful results.

Let your road trip into process mapping begin. Improve those processes that define your organization. Let's make the world an even better place…together.

Alison Smith
Westport, Connecticut

Acknowledgments

Without the inspiration, friendship, and collaboration of these people, this book would not exist.

o ACDI/VOCA – Thank you to Bill Polidoro, our CEO who empowers me to work on exciting initiatives. And I can't give enough thanks and appreciation to our global team that works tirelessly everyday towards our mission of making the world a better place. You all inspire me more than you will ever know.

o InsideNGO – Thank you to Marie McNamee for your enthusiasm and support for my workshops year after year. It is a true pleasure to work with you and your team. This book exists because of the challenge you gave me to simplify and present this topic at the awesome annual conference hosted by InsideNGO.

o Scott Vickland – Thanks for offering my name to present on this topic. I'll be sure to get you back for this.

o Beth Page – For jumping in to help me navigate the world of authoring and for getting ideas into print. Thank you, thank you!

o Marsha Moulton – Thank you for being my brutally honest collaborator and sincerest friend. There is no way I would have been as productive and effective over this last decade without our feisty and fun sessions. I treasure our time together, and look forward to our future endeavors.

o Jennifer and Vienna – My sunshine and big buddy, I simply don't have the ability to capture in words my eternal love for both of you. I appreciate each and every adventure we have together. Thanks for your support and encouragement during the presentations, workshops, and the creation of this book.

Disclaimer

This book is designed to provide information on mapping workflows and processes. It is sold with the understanding that the publisher and author are not engaged in rendering business, legal, accounting, or other professional services. If legal or other expert assistance is required, the services of a competent professional should be sought.

Every effort has been made to make this manual as complete and as accurate as possible. However, there may be mistakes, both typographical and in content. Therefore, this text should be used only as a general guide and not as the ultimate source of improving processes and workflows. Furthermore, this manual contains information that is current only up to the printing date.

The purpose of this book is to educate and entertain. The author and Promptitude Publishing shall have neither liability nor responsibility to any person or entity with respect to any loss or damage caused, or alleged to have been caused, directly or indirectly, by the information contained in this book.

If you do not wish to be bound by the above, you may return this book to the publisher for a full refund.

Introduction

We're going on a road trip!

It seems that a common part of American life is the road trip. In fact, the American Automobile Association reports that one in four Americans will take a road trip of five hours or more each year. That's a lot of traffic out on the roads. Yet, we hope that our road trip will be smooth, without incident, and that we will arrive at our destination safe and sound, right?

So it is the same for our workflow. We don't want to see traffic jams in our organizational processes. We don't want to see people having to take workaround detours because our roads are jammed and inefficient. Each time someone in your organization takes a ride on one of your processes, what kind of road trip will it be?

Workflow mapping. Process improvement. This is a critical skill set for leaders in today's complex organizations. So many processes cut across multiple departments, several locations, and – for some organizations – many countries. Often, there isn't a clear owner of the entire process. That's where you come in. Being able to facilitate a collective exercise in systematically mapping a workflow and improving it will help you to lead change in the organization.

Further, mapping and improving a workflow will save your organization money in two ways. First, of course, there are the efficiencies and benefits gained within the improved workflow itself. More outputs in less time at higher quality benefits the organization. You'll also help your organization save money by helping management avoid poor decisions such as a reorganization, new vendor, new system, or any other large scale response. As the processes become more complex and cut across many areas, these are common reactions. However, you can bypass this by taking the time to map and improve the process.

And, improving inefficient workflows will help your organization stay focused on its mission. Your organization will be able to stay focused on serving your clients. That's the strength that comes from improving a workflow.

Well, what are we waiting for? The open road calls. In five easy steps, you'll be on your way to mapping a workflow, improving a process, and leading your organization to better results.

Step 1: Define the Destination

It seems obvious, right? A road trip starts with a destination in mind. However, a destination by itself doesn't describe enough. It's the journey as much as the destination. How you get there defines the road trip as much as the destination itself. There are other elements to consider in naming your destination.

For example, let's say you chose to take a road trip to visit family in your hometown located several states away. It's not enough to describe the trip as simply *Go to My Hometown*. There are some additional questions to answer. How many hours will you drive each day? Will you occupy your time in the car with games, conversation, music, or audiobooks? Will you visit fun attractions along the way? Will you lodge in hotels or stay at campsites?

Once you've answered these questions, you will have come close to defining your road trip. Your road trip description could be *Go to My Hometown*...in three days at a casual pace of five hours of driving a day...that includes a stop at a winery and the largest ball of twine...while listening to a classic Stephen King audiobook and staying at independent roadside motels. This gives a more complete picture of what a successful road trip looks like to you. This is a Destination Description.

It's the same with process mapping.

In one international consulting firm, the staff wanted to improve their process for purchasing plane tickets. For many of us, buying a plane ticket might not be a common activity. For this firm, however, their consultants traveled around the world over half of the year. Buying a ticket was common, but inherently complicated for the firm due to a variety of factors. It was not enough to describe the destination of this process as simply *Buy a Plane Ticket*.

There were layers of complications. First, they had a variety of clients that had different reimbursement rules, such as paying for business class or preferring specific airlines. Consultants often went to risky locations that required security clearance. In watching the bottom line, the firm needed to ensure that they were paying the lowest possible price but without too many connections and long layovers. Finally, consultants often had to meet with clients on short notice and couldn't wait too long for a lengthy approval process.

In talking with a number of stakeholders on the team, we defined a more complete Destination Description:

Buy a Plane Ticket
in accordance to the client's contract
within 15% of the lowest available fair
with no more than two stops to major cities
with approval and purchase within 24 hours of request.

Doesn't that provide a more complete picture? The staff believed so. Having the definition helped the team stay focused as they went about mapping and improving the process. Another team within this international organization focused on improving the hiring process. There had been several attempts to improve various parts of the hiring process. Finally, there was a collective agreement to step back and get a complete Destination Description:

Hire a new employee
for field or headquarters
meeting all role requirements
as documented in an approved job description
that meets the client's contractual requirements
with all salary and benefits signed by the candidate
while maintaining internal equity within a global salary scale.

This organization hired consultants to work in the field on behalf of clients. For this organization, there were overlapping processes for hiring consultants in the field and staff at headquarters. Some positions had vague job descriptions, and some not at all. Various clients had different requirements for consultants working on their projects. And, since clients had final approval on positions, making sure that consultants agreed to salary and benefits *prior* to being offered to clients avoided any deal-breaking compensation conversations later. Also, as hired consultants moved across locations and to different clients, it was important that there was an equitable global scale that was fair to all.

Building Consensus

How do we get stakeholders to form a consensus around a Destination Description? Not to over simplify, but it is really nothing more than a series of patient conversations. Across the business literature, this step is often referred to as a needs analysis. And, there are plenty of tools and resources for doing this. I'm not dismissing them out of hand. I simply prefer a few open conversations with people involved with the process.

Often, people will start by describing the pain points. They will describe what the process is <u>not</u> doing right now. These are easy enough to incorporate into the Destination Description. Staff are complaining that the long approval process for airline tickets has been delaying travel. Field employees are hiring new people that don't meet all of the client's requirements. These can be articulated into the description.

But don't overlook what is already working in the process. There are specific operational standards that are currently being met (as evidenced by the existence of the process). There are organizational risks that are actively being mitigated. Be sure that these are included as well. Build off of what is working so that you are not only ensuring a more complete Destination Description, but you are also helping stakeholders recognize where they are already effective. You are generating excitement and confidence around potential improvements by showing staff that there has already been success upon which new enhancements will be established.

Speed Trap!

Just as you need to watch for speed traps on your road trip, you will need to be just as vigilant in process mapping. There seems to be an inherent desire in all teams to jump right to fixing the process. Not mapping it. Not defining the destination. Going right to the fixing. That is going way too fast and can even be dangerous.

Dangerous? Yes. There is almost nothing more debilitating to a team than to jump right into fixing only to find out that the new process still doesn't work. You spent time fixing the process. You communicated the new process to staff. You may have even spent time training staff on the new process. It might fulfill some of the organization's needs, but there are still gaps that are frustrating staff and exposing operational risks. So now what? Another fix with more communications and more training? Confidence in leadership erodes and lethargy settles in.

It will take a series of conversations and several drafts to arrive at this Destination Description. It might, no—it will—feel frustrating for the team to not be moving along faster. However, it is far better to take the time ensuring you have packed everything in your car rather than having to turn back around three hours down the road. Don't rush this process, and you'll avoid having to start over.

Driving Tips

♦ **Do it!**

As explained in the Speed Trap up above, there is a real temptation to breeze pass this step. Resist the urge. When you hold meetings about the process, keep this as the only item on the agenda. Spend the time to wordsmith the sentences and to incorporate the most important requirements of the process into the definition.

♦ **Is it complete?**

Ensure all stakeholders have contributed to the definition. This would include, of course, the primary users of the process. Also, the management team will have a series of requirements that need to be incorporated into the definition. Be sure to check with accounting and human resources as most processes have some financial and personnel considerations.

♦ **Is it clear?**

Remove ambiguity and vague descriptions from the Destination Description. Buying an airline ticket as quickly as possible is vague. Eight hours? Three days? One week? Be sure that all terms and adjectives are specific with a clear definition that is commonly understood by all stakeholders.

♦ **Is it shared?**

Not all parts of a definition will be of equal importance to an individual stakeholder, and nor should they. An accountant might be focused on the lowest price for an airline ticket whereas an employee just wants a rapid approval process. However, all stakeholders should be able to appreciate and respect all parts of the definition as being important to the organization. If there is disagreement, then spend more time on this step to work out a consensus before moving forward.

Step 2: Prepare the Vehicle

One of my first road trips was taking a convertible up the Pacific Coast Highway from Los Angeles to San Francisco. We had to pack light as we couldn't fit much in the vehicle. But that was fine as hauling luggage was not the intent of the trip. The purpose was to soak up that California sun (and perhaps to pretend we were movie stars).

Fast forward twenty years. Now my road trip involves a minivan and my family as we go to visit the grandparents over the holidays. We can load the vehicle with all of our suitcases and gifts. There is ample room for everyone to stretch out. We have the backup camera and the side sensors to let us know if a car is in our blind spot. I don't think we're turning any heads as we drive down the road. But that's okay. Our purpose is to get everyone to our destination safe and sound.

Selecting the appropriate vehicle is important. Different vehicles serve different functions. A road trip will change dramatically from an RV to a motorcycle, and from a convertible to a minivan. After selecting the vehicle, we have to prepare the vehicle. Do we need to change the oil before we go, and have we filled the gas tank? Did we check the air in the tires? Have we programmed the GPS with our stops and final destination? Have we loaded the car with our snacks and music?

Vehicles are equally important in process mapping. A process is nothing more than a route by which a task travels through to completion. The task travels through that process in a vehicle. In the *Buy a Plane Ticket* process, the task of buying a ticket will travel through multiple people and departments (and even organizations). The process might start with the traveler making a request. The request could then go to a supervisor for approval and then on to the travel agent for purchase. How does that task travel along the process? The task travels in a vehicle.

Vehicles are usually self-evident. Common vehicles are work orders, request forms, computer programs, or even an email chain. For the *Buy a Plane Ticket* process, the vehicle could be a request form. That form is initiated by the employee. This vehicle (the form) travels from the employee to the supervisor, and onward from there. The vehicle (the form) carries the task through the process.

Explicitly naming the vehicle is important as this will become the focal point of mapping and improving the workflow process. If you are having trouble identifying the vehicle, start with the very first action in the process. What action triggers the workflow? How is this action communicated? Exactly how this action travels from the first person to the next person will reveal the vehicle.

The Amazon Test

When I give workshops on process mapping, I ask participants to raise their hand if they have ever purchased an item from the online retailer Amazon. Nearly everyone raises their hand. Next, I ask them how many people have ever been to a training on how to use the Amazon website? Not a single hand in the air.

Amazon is a rather complex website. You can literally buy millions of new items from thousands of merchants. Or, you can buy used (and even sell your old stuff). You can review (and add) comments on any of these items. You can create a private wish list or publish a birthday list to share with friends. There are a plethora of gift wrapping and shipping options. You can choose from a variety of different payment methods, even signing up for the Amazon credit card. You can make this a one-time purchase or establish a recurring subscription. And, we haven't even looked at all of the digital movies, music, e-books, and audiobooks that are available – with a comprehensive search and sort feature to help you find a good recommendation or two.

Yet, many people navigate through Amazon's vehicle (the website) with great ease. Users of their workflow can select all of these options and intuitively figure out what they need to do to complete their task. It might sound like I am advocating that all people use Amazon. Not at all. I'm merely using Amazon as an example of how a vehicle can be made to facilitate a workflow (in this case, shopping).

In many organizations, what happens when a new process is created and launched? It is often followed by training. Or, if staff have not been adhering to a process, what is one of the swiftest responses? More training. Yes, I have to admit that I've been the organizer behind many of these trainings. But, wait, what does a need for training represent?

It means our vehicles have not passed the Amazon test.

When my family moved to California, our vehicle had to go through a smog test. In order to register our car, we had to have a mechanic test the exhaust of our car to ensure that it was not contributing pollution beyond a certain threshold. If the vehicle didn't pass, it wasn't allowed on the road.

Imagine if our workflow vehicles went through a similar test!

Whenever I am working with a department manager who is ready to unleash a new vehicle (requisition form, work order, or request screen), I ask for the Amazon test. Surely, the manager has already reviewed the vehicle several times. Other people who are very knowledgeable on the topic have also reviewed the vehicle. These people are important in constructing and reviewing the vehicle. However, there is one person who is often overlooked: the new employee.

I like to find one of the newest employees in the organization. Someday, this employee will need to complete the requisition form to order supplies. This employee will have to access the request screen to book an airline ticket. Without any training (just like Amazon), can the employee navigate the vehicle successfully through the process?

We literally watch over the employee's shoulder to make notes of any roadblocks or wrong turns. Too often, designers of vehicles do not realize how many assumptions they make about the knowledge of the casual user. When you work in accounting all day, you are somewhat surprised to realize that not all employees know the chart of accounts (really?). Unless the vehicle has clear instructions, the user may never reach the intended destination.

Embed Instructions

Pop quiz: what side is the gas tank on your car? When you pull into a gas station, which side do you align next to a pump: the driver or passenger side? If you were to ask me, I'm not sure I'd be able to answer this question. For my wife and me, the gas tanks for our cars are on opposite sides. But, thankfully, there is a little arrow on our gas gauges pointing to the side with the tank.

The arrow is a small example of embedding instructions.

Now that you are at the gas pump, have you ever noticed that some pumps have two hoses: one for unleaded and one for diesel? Putting diesel fuel into a standard engine would be disastrous. Sure, there are embedded instructions (the hoses are marked). But, some people are in a hurry and get distracted. To avoid this, the diesel hose nozzle is slightly larger than the unleaded – it won't fit in your gas tank. Really! Go check it out...I'll wait here.

For our workflows, we can embed instructions in the vehicle. Further, we can add protections to help users avoid common mistakes. I often observe that the instruction manual or standard operating procedures are located a distance away from the workflow. Whether this is measured in physical distance or the number of clicks, the further away the instructions are from the vehicle, the less likely they are to be used.

Electronically, we see rollover popup boxes or hyperlinks to helpful information. On forms, there needs to be more visual guidance on the information required. Providing examples is another method for embedding instructions. If there is a large amount of guidance, consider adding it at the end of the form.

Listing information in an FAQ (frequently asked questions) format with short topics and single paragraph answers will help users to quickly identify information that is most relevant. Even better, number the FAQ topics and add superscript numbers in the form itself to reference these FAQ topics at the end of the form.

FAQ Example:

For the request form to *Buy a Plane Ticket*, there could be a line that requests the preferred airline of the traveler:

PREFERRED AIRLINE[3]: _____

The number three above references an FAQ topic at the end of the form which provides additional information. An example of this topic is provided here:

FAQ #3:   Preferred Airlines. An attempt is made to book the preferred airlines of travelers. However, if the preferred airline exceeds the lowest available rate of alternate airlines by more than 15%, then the alternate airline will be booked.

You Are Here

We've all seen the maps for malls, amusement parks, zoos, and other large locations – we immediately look for the You Are Here message. On our phones or car GPS, we see the little blinking dot on our maps so we can continue on our road trip. Why not do that for our workflows?

Wherever possible, we embed the actual workflow in the vehicle. Empowering users to see the phases of the workflow helps them to understand their location. Many shopping websites display the workflow when you click on the shopping cart. It might include stages like: Review Purchases, Select Shipping, Enter Payment, Confirm Order. Anyone can understand the process. We can do this for our workflows.

Here is a simple example from a hiring screen:

Diagram 1: Hiring Workflow Status Bar

Submit	Assign	Seek	Interview	Select	Confirm	Offer

The user can observe that they are in the Interview phase of the workflow, and identify the remaining phases to be completed. They can periodically look into the workflow process to see the current status. Too often, people assume that no communication about a process means that nothing is happening. Adding this layer of transparency helps users to understand and, perhaps, appreciate the many stages of a process.

This simple tool also works for manual processes. Along the top of the form, the stages of a workflow can be listed. As a stage is completed by a person, that stage can be crossed off. Anyone seeing the form can see exactly where it is in the process. Equally important, the user can see all of the stages when starting the process.

Driving Tips

◆ **Embed Instructions**

It is a balancing act. We want the vehicle to be simple and user-friendly, but with enough guidance to help the user navigate the workflow. We don't want lengthy forms or complicated entry screens, but we need to make sure that a user can quickly get the necessary information to successfully complete the process. Hyperlinks, rollovers, FAQs, and text boxes are all helpful tools. Also, for complex processes, consider a step-by-step guide that a user could print or reference while navigating the vehicle. An example of this is any IRS form. There is the form itself, and then there is the booklet that goes with it to explain (in excruciating detail) how to complete the form. Consider such a navigation guide for your vehicle.

◆ **You Are Here**

This can be as simple as a list of the stops in a process. Visual diagrams are a great way to show a process. I openly advocate that the workflow map itself is linked to the vehicle. When people are able to see the entire process they are more likely to realize the time element and be (slightly) more patient.

◆ **Find Test Drivers**

I can't stress enough the importance of the Amazon test. Find people not familiar with the process. Watch them as they navigate the vehicle. Do this with several people, and you will quickly see the trends and common challenges. These firsthand observations will help you convince others to make changes in the vehicle.

♦ **Consider Other Vehicles**

Too often, I am on teams that just go with the vehicle that has always been used. An obvious consideration is for upgrading a manual form. Can it be converted to an electronic format? There's a downside as some electronic systems are so complex that there are programming and user interface challenges. Going the other direction, converting to a manual vehicle can be helpful. Perhaps some components of the larger workflow can be reverse engineered into a simplified manual vehicle. Perhaps not. But, ask the question and check to make sure you have the best vehicle for the process.

Step 3: Map the Route

Okay, we have a destination and a vehicle. Now, we need to define the route. My family lives near Washington, D.C. whereas my wife's extended family lives in Peoria, Illinois (something to consider carefully before choosing your lifelong partner, the town of their extended family as you will visit that town again...and again).

Each time we take this road trip we discuss the route. Which one to take? We can take a northern route through Cleveland (daughter: Rock 'n Roll Museum) across to Chicago (wife: shopping) and down to Peoria. Or, we can take a southern route through the beautiful landscape of West Virginia and up towards Indianapolis (me: largest ball of paint – no kidding, look it up) and up to Peoria. Over the years, we've found a dozen variations to these routes.

And so we must do the same with our workflow. What is the route of the process? The easiest way to do this is to simply follow the vehicle. From the initial start, follow where it goes next. Ask that person where the vehicle goes from there. And so on.

Use a visual diagram. You don't need some complicated software to make fancy boxes and linking arrows. Literally use stick figures and simple drawings to illustrate the various departments and people where the vehicle stops. People resonate very well with images. They can point and add to diagrams. In Diagram 2, you will see our sketch of the *Buy a Plane Ticket* process.

In the first stop, the employee goes to the travel agent to get a tentative itinerary and sends it to the supervisor (stop two) for approval. The supervisor then routes the itinerary through accounting (stop three) and compliance (stop four) before it is returned to the employee (stop five). In the last stop, the employee contacts the travel agent to purchase the now approved ticket.

Diagram 2: Sketch of *Buy a Plane Ticket* Process

Let your right-brain explore the artsy side. We had a little fun with the diagram. In other diagrams, people have asked to sketch their department or role in the process. It's a fun way to illustrate a workflow. The goal here is to ensure common understanding. Don't worry you left-brainers, we'll make it official looking in the next chapter.

Don't get bogged down into details. Just like a list of cities, list the stops that the vehicle travels throughout the process. Don't get trapped down into the explicit tasks and activities within each stop. This is another value of the visual diagram. It keeps you out of the weeds. Using a narrative-based description will morph into a lengthy document that few will read. Be a mapmaker instead!

Capture the process as it is now, workarounds included. Some people may explain that they think the process 'should' go this way.

Don't include it. Or, they will explain that they are planning to 'add' a stop. *Don't include this one either.* The operating procedures may dictate a certain stop, but no one actually does it. *Nope, keep it off your map.* Our goal is to make a clear map of the actual route.

As straightforward as this step might sound, be flexible. I am often surprised as to what I think would be a simple process is actually rather complex. And, for many processes, few (if any) people know the entire route. This is a reason for so many process challenges. Many workflows cut across multiple departments, several cities, and – for some organizations – even a few countries. How could any one person know the entire route?

Many people only know from where the vehicle arrives, and where it departs to next. Don't be surprised if you get conflicting information as people share stops further along the process from where they sit. This is why it is important for you to follow the vehicle to each stop. You'll likely re-write your process several times as you interview more and more people involved in the workflow.

Once you have created your map, go back and review it with everyone involved in the process. This is a map of the process as it is now. Your goal here is to validate the map. Have you correctly defined the route? Can anyone reading the map clearly follow the route? This small action goes a long way in building a common understanding. We'll refine this map in the next chapter.

Driving Tips

♦ **Bring a Pencil**

I am mostly using this term figuratively, but bring out the pencils if you have them. The point here is that you will likely re-write and re-write the process map as you follow the vehicle. It is not only that people will give conflicting information, but some processes have a complexity that will require some creativity. This complexity often comes out from If/Then scenarios. Example: If the purchase is over a certain amount, then it must go to the CFO for approval. Another example: If the product does not meet quality standards, then it must go to the design team. As you follow these various detours, you'll need to be flexible in editing your map.

♦ **Visit the Stops**

We are in a fast-paced world. Emails and instant messages are so efficient, right? However, I find that sitting with each person on the stop is much more effective than simply emailing or calling people, especially when dealing with the sensitive topic of workflow. After all, this stop on the workflow map represents someone's duty, function, or responsibility. We don't want to come across as glib or insensitive. Also, since we are mapping this workflow to improve it, we want to be sensitive to their concerns. As much as possible, we will likely need to collaborate with all people involved with the workflow to make improvements. Spending time upfront will go a long way in building relationships for improving the process.

Another benefit of spending face-to-face time is allowing participants to see the entire map. I am continually amazed to watch people read over a process that they've been involved in for years, but never knew all of the stops on the route that came through their department. Not only are people informing your map, your map is also informing them.

♦ **Stay Out of the Weeds**

There is a temptation to get into a deeper discussion of the details that occur within each stop. When you engage people about their duties, they may be interested in showing you all the various activities that they conduct. This is important, but not yet. Your goal here is to know that the vehicle makes a stop here, and then goes on to the next stop.

Step 4: Describe the Stops

When I think back to the ancient technologies we used on road trips, you know…way back…to 2008 or so, I recall that all we had was MapQuest. (Of course, prior to that, we had the folding paper maps. I tried explaining this to my young daughter, but she thinks I'm pulling her leg.) Today, many cars and nearly every smartphone provides directions. We still occasionally print a MapQuest set of instructions for road trips – perhaps a bit nostalgic or in case of gadget failure.

I appreciate the succinct directions of MapQuest. *Turn left on South Street. Merge onto I-74 west. Take Exit 5A onto Main Street.* These are very clear. They are concise. They are unambiguous. GPS devices follow this same format in providing clear directions.

We need to define each stop in the workflow with the same simple instructions. I challenge myself and people mapping workflows to define each stop in just three or four words, with the first word being a verb. For our *Buy a Plane Ticket* process, we see the following stops being defined:

- Employee   Submit travel request
- Travel Agent   Create tentative booking
- Employee   Send to supervisor
- Supervisor   Approve trip purpose
- Accountant   Confirm available budget
- Compliance   Ensure compliance to policy
- Employee   Send approved request
- Travel Agent   Purchase ticket
- Employee   Send copy to supervisor
- Supervisor   File and forward
- Accountant   Accrue travel expense

For each of the stops in our *Buy a Plane Ticket* process map (from Step 3), we have now defined what occurs at each stop in just three or four words. Don't give long and drawn out explanations. Think MapQuest. Provide just enough information to capture the primary purpose of the stop. You may find that the employees at each stop of the process want to provide a lot more detail. It's not that we don't appreciate all of the additional information, it is just not necessary at this time.

It's time to organize our workflow map (cheers from the left-brainers). Take a piece of legal paper or even a flipchart, and create the following diagram:

Diagram #3: Swim Lane Map

Next, place each of the stops from the workflow map into one of the lanes you have created. After placing the stops, you'll see why this is often referred to as a Swim Lane map. Each of the departments or employees look like they are about to swim across a pool. Below is an example from the *Buy a Plane Ticket* process:

Diagram #4: Swim Lane Map with Stops

With this structure, we can indicate the direction of the workflow and insert the definitions of each stop:

Diagram #5: Completed Swim Lane Map

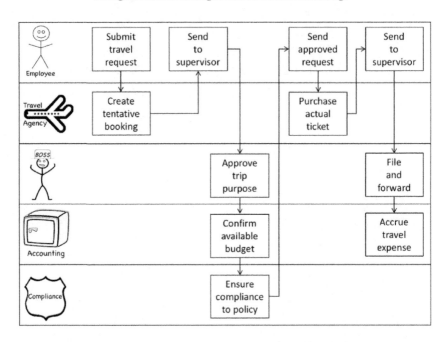

With this *Buy a Plane Ticket* diagram, we have provided a clear picture of how a workflow process is completed. We can see all of the stops, the order of the stops, and what occurs at each stop. We can look at one particular person or department to see how many times a single workflow comes through them. We can see how many stops overall.

To create the Swim Lane diagram, it is helpful if you can get everyone into one room. Draw a Swim Lane diagram on a flipchart. Use sticky notes to define what happens at each stop. Remember, stay focused on describing what happens now, not any desired future state or a description of what the policy manual says it should be.

If you can't get everyone in a room (or onto a call), then come back around and talk to each of the participants again. You might be asking, "Why didn't I do this while I was completing Step 3?" That is, while we were making a map of the process, why didn't we ask them then what happened at that stop?

I offer two reasons: clean map and big picture. By focusing on the map in Step 3, you are focused on identifying the stops. You provide a clean map that is very clear on all of the stops. If you start asking about what happens at each stop, there is a temptation to get pulled down into the weeds.

Also, when you have all of the participants reviewing the overall big picture, they might be better able to articulate what they do in the perspective of the big picture. Without the process map, an accountant might say that she looks up the general ledger, reviews the pending accruals, and calculates the budget available for buying a ticket. Instead, by looking at a completed process map from Step 3, she can articulate her role as confirming available funds. The completed map from Step 3 gives her a broader perspective on how to communicate her role here in Step 4.

For these reasons, I strongly recommend that people complete Step 3 (map the route) before moving onto Step 4 (describe the stops with a swim lane diagram). It will keep you more focused on collecting the critical information you need for each step of mapping a workflow.

Driving Tips

♦ **Keep It Simple**

Remember, only use three or four words. The first word is a verb. I've yet to find a stop in a workflow that couldn't be simplified so that anyone could understand it. That's not to say that the task is simple, just that describing it is simple.

♦ **Shift Swim Lanes**

Swim lanes can get complicated, particularly if a workflow goes back and forth between a few departments. It might make it easier to move the order of swim lanes so that those departments that interact more frequently are closer together.

♦ **Create Multiple Pages**

For long workflows with numerous stops, consider defining it in phases (after all, some road trips are multiple days!). Create a separate page for each phase. For the *Hire an Employee* process, the first phase could be Approval (write job description, check budget, etc.) – which could have a dozen stops. The second phase could be Selection (place ad, interview, etc.) – which would have another dozen stops. The third phase could be Hiring (check background, make offer, etc.) with the remaining stops.

♦ **Merge Stops within a Department**

This one is a bit of a judgment call. Some workflows might make a stop in a department that has several internal stops within that department. For the *Buy a Plane Ticket* process, the travel agency receptionist receives the request from the employee and logs it for the travel agent. The travel agent identifies a potential flight, and sends it to a rate desk for approval. The rate desk approves it and sends it to the receptionist, who sends it back to the employee.

In this example, there are multiple internal stops. However, for our workflow, we can capture all of this under the travel agent as "Purchase Ticket." Do we really need to list all of the internal stops within this? Usually, no. However, you might find this is an important level of detail for other stops in your workflow. This will occur if there is a perception of too much time at a specific stop, and that these functions need to be further detailed. Or, there might be a question as to clarifying the various internal stop responsibilities. In these cases, you could list them. Or, list the one single stop on your main Swim Lane diagram, and then a separate sheet for the multiple internal stops.

Step 5: Clarify the Roles

There are four critical roles on a road trip. (Want to take a moment and see if you can name all four?) First, there is the driver who is *responsible* for the navigation of the vehicle. Next to the driver, we have the co-pilot. This person *approves* what the driver does (at least, that's how it happens in my family): how fast we're going, how close we're following the car in front of us...you get the idea.

In the back of the vehicle, we have the passengers who *contribute* to the decisions being made. They help determine how long to the next stop, what music to listen to, what temperature to set, and so on. Finally, the last role is that of the family and friends we'll see along the way. For them, we need to *inform* them of when we'll arrive, if we will have already eaten, and how long we're staying.

If you've survived the metaphor, we can strip it away now to pull out the four critical roles in any workflow. It is commonly referred to in the process mapping literature by its acronym RACI, which represents:

Responsible: person responsible to see task through to completion

Approver: anyone who has go/no-go authority

Contributor: anyone who contributes to the final product

Informed: anyone who needs to be notified at any point within the process, but does not contribute to the final product

Responsible

There is one person who is ultimately responsible for the successful completion of the workflow. Too often, this is left undefined and falls onto the user by default. This is commonly found for those processes that cut across multiple departments. Many individuals contribute to the process, but there is not a clearly designated person who is ultimately responsible. For the *Book a Plane Ticket* process mapped in Step 4, it would appear that it is up to the employee to follow-up with the various departments to ensure completion. We've all been there, right?

Therefore, it is important to identify this person, someone to assume clear ownership. If a process is mainly driven within a department, then the Responsible person will likely be someone within that department. For those processes cutting across multiple departments, consider someone who isn't even involved in the process. For the *Buy a Plane Ticket* process, the organization I assisted identified a manager who oversees operations to be the Responsible person. Not a single stop of the workflow comes to this manager. This provides an independent view of the workflow process.

Approver

An Approver is anyone who has go/no-go authority. In other words, this person can stop the process. There is usually an inordinate amount of Approvers in a process. Some approval is fundamental in any process, but there are often too many Approvers. For example, let's look at the *Buy a Plane Ticket* process from Step 4. It's straightforward that the supervisor is an Approver. But so is the accountant who is confirming if there are enough funds. The compliance officer is also an Approver by determining if the trip has been booked according to company policy. That's three Approvers within this process.

Approvers are often added over time to a process. At some historical point in the past, there was a failure in a process that resulted in a loss for the organization. At that point, someone was inserted into the workflow to review all future transactions to avoid such a failure from happening again. This may have been an appropriate short-term action until a deeper analysis could be conducted as to the cause of the failure. However, these temporary inserts often become permanent. A larger process with multiple departments might have multiple Approvers within each of the departments. Participants who review an overall process map are often surprised when counting the total number of Approvers in a process.

Contributor

A Contributor is anyone who adds value to the final product of the workflow. The final product is different before and after it has stopped with the Contributor. This is, in effect, where the work gets done on the specific workflow.

For the *Hire an Employee* process, this would include the person writing the job description, the person posting the advertisement, the person conducting the interview, the person doing the background checks, and the person making the offer to the candidate. Each of these people completing these tasks would be a Contributor.

Informed

Anyone who needs to be informed about the workflow process is consider an informed stakeholder. This person may need to be informed within the workflow process or upon the completion of the process. This person does not contribute to the final product. This person does not have go/no-go authority.

For the *Buy a Plane Ticket* process, there could be a receptionist that is informed so as to re-direct incoming calls for staff away on travel. For the *Hire an Employee* process, there could be an operations person that needs to be informed to identify a workspace. Neither of these people contribute to the workflow itself, but require information from that workflow.

Assign a Letter

For this final step in mapping a workflow process, we need to assign a letter to each person in the workflow process. Let's review our Swim Lane diagram as an example:

Diagram #6: Swim Lane Map with RACI Roles

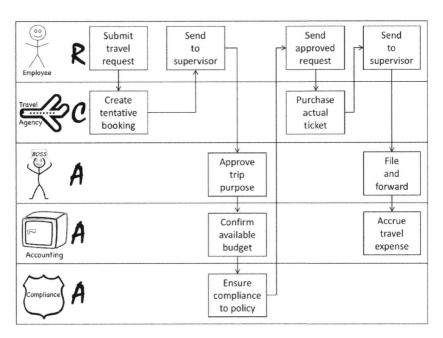

Responsible. In this example, the employee appears to be ultimately responsible to ensure that the process is completed. As explained earlier, this is not recommended. When the user is the person responsible, you will find more quality errors and discover more workarounds. Also, there will be no learning from an overall review of transactions to find inefficiencies and improvements.

Approvers. For the approvers, we see that there are three: supervisor, accountant, and compliance officer. Any one of these individuals can stop the process. There may be good reasons for this. Later in this chapter, we will strategize how to reduce the number of approvers without losing quality control and appropriate risk mitigation.

Contributors. The travel agent is the lone contributor in this example. The travel agent creates a tentative booking and purchases the final ticket. These actions contribute to the final product.

Informed. In this example, no informed stakeholders have been identified. However, as in the example provided earlier, there could be a receptionist that is informed so as to re-direct incoming calls for staff away on travel.

Driving Tips

♦ **Confirm the Responsible Person**

There might be a manager or person who raises their hand and says that they are Responsible. Sometimes, they are responsible for the vehicle. Or, they are responsible for a core function of the workflow. We can only assign the 'R' to the person who ensures that all stops are completed within a workflow. It is frequently absent when there are multiple departments. There is an 'R' for each department, but not one overall person responsible. In these cases, it falls – by default – onto the user.

Where possible, identify someone who is not an active stop within the workflow itself. This person can provide an independent view of the process by collecting feedback from users, reviewing traffic jams, and identifying vehicle improvements. Particularly for cross-department processes, an independent person can facilitate discussions to review the process.

♦ **Watch for Hidden Approvers**

Approvers aren't always explicitly self-identified. Their function might be couched in language as "I confirm..." or "I check..." to describe their role. These are all actions of Approvers. Approvers not only confirm and check, they also authorize, endorse, review, consent, and double-check. These are all Approver functions.

♦ **Reduce Number of Approvers**

There is a balance between efficiency and real risk. Approvers are primarily positioned to limit risk to the organization. For processes where failure can result in serious loss such as personnel safety or large finances, then Approvers are critical.

If the risks are smaller or less frequent, consider removing the Approver.

Also, thresholds are a common practice for reducing Approvers. Financial thresholds are common in procurement: the higher the amount being spent, the higher the level of authority required. Non-financial thresholds can also be established. For example, perhaps employees that have worked more than three years won't need a supervisor's approval for certain tasks. Or, travel to a country with a low level security risk will not need prior security authorization. Although you might not be able to (nor want to) remove an Approver altogether, finding an acceptable threshold will reduce the frequency that an Approver is involved in a workflow.

♦ **Find Shortcuts around Contributors**
There are Contributors, and there are Contributors. Huh? There are those Contributors that are truly shaping the final product. There are also Contributors that are adding helpful information, but it is information that could be referenced by the user.

Using the Amazon example again, the person who runs through the warehouse to retrieve your products is a Contributor. Imagine if you had to send your order to someone else who looked up the shipping fees, and then that person sent you an email with your options. Well, yes, that sounds silly. We all know that there is a reference table for you to select shipping preference and rate. You don't need to go through someone else. However, someone behind the scenes is managing that shipping cost information. Many of our workflows, though, include people who contribute information that could also be referenced by the user.

Let's take an example. In the *Buy a Plane Ticket* process, the accountant is checking to see if there are sufficient travel funds. Could a link to the budget be provided for the supervisor? The supervisor could insert the budget and remaining amounts into the request form to demonstrate that this has been checked. Accounting maintains the books, but doesn't need to be involved in the workflow. Or, for the *Hire an Employee* process, the process could include a stop where it goes to the Human Resources department to determine the salary. But, what if the positions are assigned to grade levels with salary ranges? Human Resources can maintain the table, but doesn't need to do this task in the workflow process for each individual hire.

Scrutinize what the Contributors are adding to the process. First, confirm that they really aren't Approvers-in-disguise. Second, see if what they are providing could be accessed directly by the user. The Contributor can and should maintain the content being referenced, and will no longer need to be in the process itself. Just confirm that any information you are now requiring the user to access passes the Amazon test. That is, be sure that what you are asking the user to do is simple and straightforward.

♦ **Passive vs. Active Informed**
An effective workflow will balance risk mitigation with process efficiency. Fewer stops without reducing quality or raising risk is the goal. One strategy is to ask Approvers to switch to being Informed. That is, rather than the process having to make a stop at their desk, they can just monitor the traffic as it goes by. This allows them to monitor events without the process being stopped. That's a tricky negotiation that requires a discussion of the perceived risks.

For those who are Informed (including ex-Approvers), the next decision point is to determine Active or Passive informing. Active informing is a message that comes to the person at a trigger point in the process. This is typically an email, report, or other message that is sent to the person. For example, a supervisor could receive an email whenever an employee sends a request to a travel agent in the *Buy a Plane Ticket* process. This could replace the supervisor's need to be an Approver in the process.

Passive informing requires the person to look up the information in an established and easily searchable table, chart, database, or other resource. For the *Buy a Plane Ticket* process, all requests sent to the travel agent could be stored in a table. The supervisor (or any other stakeholder) can review the table at any time to review activities.

As a workflow person, I prefer building Passive communications to maximize workflow efficiency. However, this needs to be assessed against the level of risk. A general rule for risk levels:

- High risk: Approver
- Medium risk: Active Informed
- Low risk: Passive Informed

Changing Roles

By applying the tips above, we can make specific improvements to the *Buy a Plane Ticket* process. Here is the process, and we can make the following changes as numbered on the chart:

Diagram 7: Swim Lane with Identified Improvements

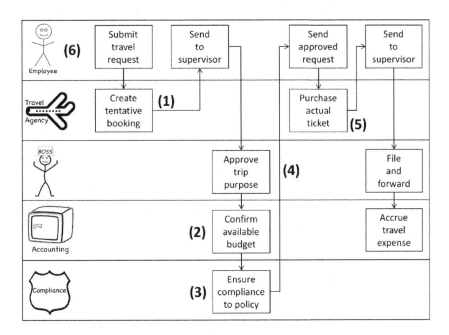

(1)   We modify the vehicle to include the name of the supervisor. After the travel agent books the tentative ticket, a simple re-routing here sends it directly to the supervisor. Now, the employee does not have to send it to the supervisor.

(2)   We provide a simple lookup table for the supervisor to check the remaining budget for travel. The accountant maintains these tables for all supervisors. This change removes the accountant as an Approver in the process.

(3) The compliance officer was required to ensure that the tentative ticket followed company polices. The compliance officer established a clear checklist for the travel agent, and renegotiated the travel agent contract to include this quality check in their services. The compliance officer was removed as an Approver from the process.

(4) With the accountant and compliance officer removed from the process, the now approved travel request travels from the supervisor directly back to the travel agent. The travel agent books the ticket.

(5) All booked tickets were catalogued in a simple database. This enabled the supervisor to review trips at any time. The accountant could accrue travel costs at any time. The compliance officer could conduct spot audits to ensure that trips met company policy. This shortened the workflow process.

(6) The organization identified the operations manager to serve as the Responsible person for the workflow. This removes the employee from having to be the default Responsible person for the process. In this role, the operations manager chose active notification for all requests that went unanswered for 24 hours. The manager used passive notification on a monthly basis to review all trips booked for any issues.

Our new workflow map is as follows:

Diagram 8: Simplified Workflow

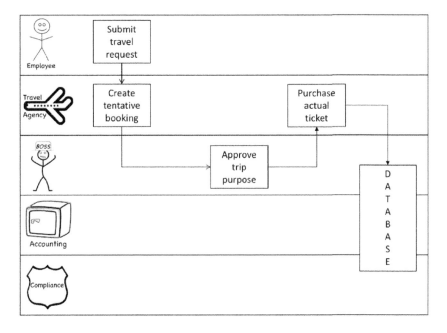

Final Driving Tips

Go slow, don't steamroll

If you are working to improve a workflow process, there can be a temptation to move quickly into fixing the workflow. I've seen this temptation increase when I or others are 'outsiders' to the process. That is, it's obvious to us what needs to be changed. However, processes emerge from complex organizational history. No one has the whole story. Take your time to discover what's going on.

Also – and this can't be understated – you are dealing with the primary functions of employees. This is their job, passion, and livelihood. Treat the topic of workflow sensitively. People are often glad to get rid of unnecessary work. However, no one likes to hear that their efforts are not needed. So, go slow and steady to ensure that everyone is coming along with you.

Compromise when necessary

Power is often diffused in workflows that cut across multiple departments. There are clear department managers. But how do you rank priorities that cut across department lines? It can get sensitive and tricky here. And, depending on individual personalities and department priorities, it can be difficult to ask people to give up their Approver status. It might be a challenge asking a Contributor to put their information into a reference table for users to access. It's change, and all people react differently to it. Compromise where you need to, and consider a detour (see next tip).

Ask people to test a new way temporarily

If you are talking with someone who is hesitant to try a new way either because of a perceived increase in risk or a loss of control, ask them to test the new way. This can be done over a period of time, or just for the first batch of transactions to come through the process. Agree to sit and review the first set together. Identify where the issues are and see if the workflow can't be improved. If the trial period is successful, consider expanding the time period between reviews until the change can be made permanent.

Remind people where they are going

As the amount of change and tension increases, continually remind people of the Destination Description (from Step 1). Although the proposed process might be new, different, and a little uncomfortable, remind them it is worth the ride if the end is achieved. Check the outputs of the workflow process to determine if the end is, in fact, being achieved. If it is, let people know that the changes are working.

If participants or stakeholders of the workflow are expressing concerns about an element of the output that is <u>not</u> included in your Destination Description, then you will need to modify the Destination Description. For example, in the *Buy a Plane Ticket* process, perhaps travelers complained about not getting their preferred airlines in order to collect frequent flyer miles. The destination description would need to be modified to represent this additional requirement while ensuring that the other priorities (such as price) are still fulfilled.

Be sure to involve and handover to the R

If the R (that is, the person who will be Responsible for the workflow) is evident from the beginning of the process, be sure that this person is involved in all mapping activities and discussions. Often, this person is not identified until the middle of the workflow mapping exercise. As soon as the R has been identified, engage that person.

If that person is you, which is likely since you are reading this book, then be sure you have established lots of Active informing for the initial launch (yes, this is opposite of what was advised for Approvers). You want to be informed of all activities in the beginning. As you gain trust in the process and the quality of the outputs, then you can shift to more Passive informing with a routine review.

Hold onto the Swim Lane diagram, monitor the performance of the workflow, collect feedback from users driving the vehicle, and review this with the participants in your workflow. Doing this on a routine basis can increase the performance of your workflow and benefit your organization.

Good luck on your road trip!

Printed in Great Britain
by Amazon